Dedication

This book is dedicated to the great vine of life; Jesus Christ.

Lord, you are worth all the praise and thanksgiving.

Acknowledgments

Many people have played a part in inspiring me to write and publish this book of firsts as well as helped me through this process by inspiring, motivating, and mentoring my spirit.

I first off want to give a huge thank you to a wonderful dear friend of mine; Diane Pullano. Diane I cannot thank you enough for our lovely conversations involving the beauty of this world and the importance of love. Your insights and belief in me have moved me to grow stronger and stand taller, as well as grow in confidence in faith. I utmostly cannot thank you enough for the typewriter you've gifted me for my 20th birthday. Without the typewriter I cannot say this would have been possible. Thank you for the encouraging, loving words that you've always spoken over me. I next give thanks to my church, SOPAR. Though we are small in numbers, we are big in spirit.

I want to give a huge thank you to Judah Angeles and Trinity Angeles. Thank you for always speaking words of life over me and keeping me in prayer. Your love has never gone unseen, and your grace is utmostly deeply appreciated. Through your teachings, I have grown to be a stronger, taller, smarter woman in faith and to walk with deeper wisdom in this life. Thank you for your fervent dedication and love for Jesus, it has ignited the fire within me to grow deeper with Him and to want more of Him. Thank you both for being the spiritual mother and father I have always prayed for since my walk with Jesus began. You both have aided me in growing in stature and love, which is the greatest gift of all. You both have played a huge role in the restoration of my faith which guided me back to Jesus in my darkest moments. Apostle Miracle, I want to thank you for your powerful prayers filled with deep love and passion for Jesus, it has helped me understand the importance and power of prayer. Charisma, I want to thank you for your intercessory over my life and for your words of life over me. Thank you for encouraging me and mentoring me with the Word of God; you have helped me understand the power of God's Word. Zion, thank you for inspiring me to continue following my passion for writing as well as inspiring me to take my passions more seriously to form my visions into a reality. You have helped me understand the importance of creation through vision. Thank you for the photograph you have taken of me, now it is my first author's photo! Mom, thank you for doing your best to raise me. You have given me the best gift of all: life. If it weren't for you this would not be possible.

Thank you for speaking of Jesus and taking us to church as kids. It has always ignited a fire within me that I now know has been the Holy Spirit. Your prayers and faith in Jesus has led me to receive Him to revive my spirit. Thank you for teaching me that anything is possible through faith. Your love and grace towards others has been the greatest testimony of Jesus's love. Thank you for loving Jesus mom, never let His love go. I now want to give thanks to my team with Global Publishers.

I am immensely grateful for you all working with me to make my vision a reality! I thank you all for being patient with my vision and my work. Thank you, Brian Wilson for managing the creation of this book for it to be published! Thank you to the editors and proofreaders for the formatting and adjustment of this book. Thank you, Emily Williams for connecting with me and keeping me in touch with the process of the finishing of this book! I appreciate and thank you all for your dedication to making this book of poetry a wonderful reality!

About the Author

Mariah Schneider is a passionate follower of Christ. She was raised by her mother, along with two of her siblings, in Los Angeles, California. She is a fervent helper of many via YouTube creating Christ-filled content to help aid many on their walk with Christ. Mariah is 21 years old who is a teacher by day and follows her passion for writing by night. This is Mariah's first published book and will not be her last. She is currently in college, completing her BA in Child Development. She has a passion for helping people and shining Christ's light on others. She is a committed member of SOPAR (Church/fellowship), which has aided her in her growth and knowledge of Jesus. Mariah has always enjoyed writing poetry since she was young. It was not until she got deeper into her relationship with Christ, as well as moments of deep healing, that she was pulled to get back into poetry. Mariah has used poetry through many moments of healing from trauma, broken relationships, growth/restoration in self, as well as gaining a deeper understanding of the eternity of life with Jesus. She enjoys running, reading, working with children, creating fun-loving moments with others as well as taking walks in nature.

Introduction

This collection of poems, prayers, and reflections has been written during seasons of healing, growth, and spiritual transformation. Each piece reflects moments of deep connection with God, where faith and love served as guiding lights through life's challenges. These writings are an offering to encourage and inspire, showing how God's presence can bring comfort, strength, and renewal.

Life is filled with trials, but it is often in these difficult moments that we find the greatest opportunities for growth. As the Bible says in **Psalm 34:18**: *"The Lord is close to the brokenhearted and saves those who are crushed in spirit."* This collection seeks to capture the hope and peace found in God's love, even in times of struggle.

The poems explore themes of divine love, spiritual growth, romantic longing, and the journey of life. Each section offers a glimpse into a different aspect of the human experience, always pointing back to the faith that sustains and strengthens us. As written in **Isaiah 40:31**: *"But those who hope in the Lord will renew their strength. They will soar on wings like eagles; they will run and not grow weary, they will walk and not be faint."* These words remind us of the power of faith to carry us forward.

Poetry has a unique way of expressing what words alone often cannot—emotions, questions, and truths that resonate deeply within the heart. Through these pages, I hope you will find encouragement to draw closer to God, reflecting on His love and grace in your life. In **John 8:12**, Jesus says, *"I am the light of the world. Whoever follows me will never walk in darkness, but will have the light of life."* It is my prayer that these writings shine that light into your heart.

Thank you for joining me on this journey of faith and reflection. May you find peace, joy, and a deeper understanding of God's love as you read.

Mariah Schneider

Ezekiel 8:4

"Like the appearance of a rainbow in a cloud on a rainy day, so was the appearance of the brightness all around it. This was the appearance of the likeness of the glory of the Lord."

A Thank You to Jesus

Hi Jesus, I wanted to thank You for waking me up, giving me this life. New air in my lungs every moment and second. I woke up with a sense of refreshment, a peace in what is new and what has been restored. The birds are chirping, the sun is shining, and best of all: Your mercies are made new every morning.

I have been feeling this peace for the past couple of weeks. Everything's in place. You are doing lots of work, and I am just trusting You with it all. I don't know what is to come next, but I know You're with me—that's all I need to know.

In the Heavens

The gate was open.
Nobody entered.
The House was empty.
They were to dwell in the pastures up above.
Unfortunate causes led them below.

Before, I thought it was just a choice.
The truth is, the devil did everything in his power for them to not enter.
He took the souls and made them lost.
Only the strong have lived.

The ungodly lied in the ears.
Deception was whispered in their ears, causing them to sin,
Causing the religious folk to be hindered.
The religious were the worst speakers.
For the religious spirits led many astray.

As pigs led pigs, the religion engulfed the dark.
The weaker those lost souls became, and as he fed,
the goats continued on...

To ascend up in Heaven, with His army of angels, He captured the bondage and made them free.
The light has overcome, and the darkness could not comprehend it.

I am done running. I am done hiding. It is time I take my seat where I belong.

In His presence, within His embrace.

I am taking my space, I am taking my breath.

He will not forsake me, I know so.

Everlasting mercy, eternal love.

Prayer of Heart

I wake up with such wonder and awe that You are my Savior.
With everlasting thanksgiving, I bow to You with my heart.
For the restoration, the great peace.
You are the Great, beyond man and time.
You are the beholder of my existence.

The Movement of Spirit

The winds whoosh, and the rains fall as they click to the ground,
I think to myself, what an easeful sound.
I know the part may not play the character's finest wishes,
But as this rain falls, I am reminded we're not always given the start.

We have to fall as rain does, so we may come as one as a rainbow with the colors of all.

I am yet so happy to see what has been made by Thee.
The glorious hand set out above,
I will not give up what is waiting for them.
In the hands of the Beholder, I leave it,
But my work I will get done.
It is my desire that He and I shall become one.

Life of the Human

The birds sing,
Waking the life of creation beneath the soil.
The breath flows continually within the human spirit.
Ever flowing,
Time embraced.

In a mother's womb, the life waits for battle,
For love,
For eternal connection.

To be seen, to be cherished.
One's desire with their heart on fire.
Everything received is what you make of it.
Create what you must.
Cherish what you will,
It will not be your last.

The ending forms a new beginning.
So loosen your hand, my dear,
Loosen your grasp.
The world is yonder, and there is much to ponder.

Everyone plays a part in the entanglement of breath,
The dance that we must play a rhythm to,
The sound that we must run to.

When our time comes, we will know then
That what we reaped is what we have sown.

That every fear, every tear, every grasp merely comes to a stop,
Eventually.

What I have to say is,
Take this time, dear, hold it near.
Do not make a decision upon a tear or fear.
But darling, oh darlin', let it be clear.

That the journey you take on is yours.
There will be laughs, cries, death.
But despite all, hold this moment tight.

The Birth of the Spirit Within

My mind seems to be curious. In awe, I look around,
asking questions.
I wonder if I should take them seriously.
I began to pray, and what I felt, you could not pay.
A tiny beam of faith from within clung onto the Highest. How could you know?
How could you see it? You could not know.
The sound was drowning Him out.
You ran until you were met with the reflection of yourself.
You had to stop looking,
it drove you mad.
The thought of your existence clung you to the pity of this earth.
Until then, you understood the tales written:
The nations were sensible. The land is cursed.
That what is yours cannot be taken.
What is dear to you will be your safe haven.
You prayed as the night called you into a deep sleep.
You feared what you now know may slip through in a dream,
That you would wake to the cluelessness of your mind.
That time itself will be fatal.
That what you know now will be the departure. The departure of what is seen, of what is believed.

To begin watering the seeds of growth.

For your eyes to be opened to a new cloth,

The sweet smells of life, to be restored.

The continuing of your dance, your song, your love. And so it was taken,

This world is vanity, but let you not be forsaken.

You were loved through it all, as the eternal flow of the breath passes.

Accept the dance, the rhythm, you are set free, in one, to be.

The Collision of Faith and Wisdom

There is a God in Heaven. We know this for certain.
All creation tells us so. As the sun shines,
My spirit will have faith in the Almighty. He is a wonderful God.
Brokenness brings us closer to His love. Emptiness brings us to His fullness.
He is our God.
He will not forsake us. He is a great God.
All I have been through has only taught me how short this life is.
How fleeting it is as a speck of dust.
To receive life is to understand death.
Life is a string blowing in the wind.
You may not know where it is to go, but you know it is going.
So His spirit must reign through.

Prayer for His Glory to Shine

I will give unto You what I may have to.

There is an end to everything, even the sun stops shining.

Through it will pass as He comes unto.

His love will shine through it all.

I don't know for certain what lies beyond my path,

But Lord, I give it unto You.

Whatever You will, my God.

I am lifted up, shining in the light of Your glory.

Pour out Your love as we sing, *holy, holy, holy.*

The Beginning of Love from Above

What is it to be in love? Is it the caress of a hand?
The words of endearment?
The thoughts that roam through my mind?
The giddy feeling I get at the thought of seeing you?
The look in your eyes tells me thousands of words.
Without a spoken word,
My prayers lead to a cry, a cry for the flesh that is weak.
A cry for the spirit to be raised from this body of mine.
Be not afraid, for the weak are being made strong.
For the castles are being built.
The time is coming when you and I shall meet and have a very fine greet.
Smile on, past the muck.
Your heart will be joyous,
Your mouth will speak of power and love.
So go on after your somber heart.
Your youthful cry, out to the sky.
I never knew what it was to be loved until I felt His embrace from above.
He cured my somber heart,
Turned my sorrows into song.
He molded my wretched hands to give when I felt no will to live.

His love caressed my heart,

His patience lifted me up and gave me a new start.

A Letter to Jesus

Hi Lord, I love You.

Sometimes my heart aches from past hurt, but Lord, I know this heart is healing.

I know so.

Thank You for Your love.

Merciful Father.

Thank You for this time, this moment, this youth.

Thank You for what's around me, the passage of time, the experience, the coming and going.

Everflowing of life.

You're with me, I must be content with now.

My own.

Thank You.

It's Wrapped in a Vintage Bow

He has given it to you, most, if not all, this. So make do.

The Choices of Life

I once thought life was just a role we play,
A suit or dress we wear as we work and earn.
All for the money's expense.
That the only joy to be found was to fall in love for a short time and continue on.
Smile for the picture, awe at the cute baby, pet the friendly dog coming your way.
Cry at the heartache, grow stronger because of it,
Quit your boring job, get that degree, or drop out... it's your choice. But is it?
Continue on... feeling happy for a time, visiting that beautiful place, drinking that good wine and caviar.
Attend the funerals, greet old friends, or don't. Again, it's your choice...
Yes, marry that girl, yes, get that car, yes, take that job you have wanted.
Go have lunch with that client who's been bothering you.
No, don't cheat on your wife, she loves you, and you need her.
No, don't get that house you can't afford.
No, don't take that loan out...
Stop drinking, you're messing it up, everything we created.
You're tearing the beautiful life apart...

That, ladies and gentlemen, is a representation of vanity.
Of shooting at mid-air, living by a picture.

No purpose, just feeling.

But see, the devil comes to seek, kill, and destroy.

No matter where you are, it can either get better or worse.

It all starts with the choice.

The choice that can lead you to life or death.

What will it be?

Again, it's your choice.

To Be Lifted by Him

The older I get, the more I reflect on the past.
For a while, I was held back, in my own grip. Voices around made me somber.
I knew my strength but didn't see the point.
Why is it that I was less happy with lots of people but happier with less?
Abuse began to taunt me.
My eyes began to open, the light began to shine.
There was nothing I could do but accept the unknown.
After all, aren't I alone? Aren't we all? I let go.

Once I did, I began to show, and my surroundings were dim, but I was my truest self, who He called me to be.
My wings spread, I did not stop, not for a moment did I look down.
But I continued on. My knowledge felt as if it surpassed even the wisest of folk, even the eldest.
I couldn't do what most have done to me.
But I hold dear to love because I know it is all I must ever need.

A boy broke my heart. I fell dearly.
I let go of my sight; my vision was blind.
I wanted love, and for that, I gave my own.
Write, write I must. I have my wings back.

I am fully intact. Yet again, I choose to give back.
I will never give up. I know love will win. It must.

Yes, I was then.
But now, I am me. I can see.
My focus is aligned, my goals are in sight.
My arms are putting up the fight.
The love is giving its shine. I will continue on.
Flying. It's not about my breath but about Him who gave it.
They are desperate for love.
To be seen and caressed. To be looked upon.
Who will be there? Who will give it?
It must be... God Himself.

Music is the Highest Praise

Jesus is the Highest name above all creation.

Could you hear the shout of the Heavens rising above all?

My Heart Shall Be in Him

My love, my love, I won't give my heart to you.
For it is with the Lord, resting in His embrace.
For He is the only one I trust. How could I not?
Louder than the cries, louder than the ones with pride.
For He has given me life.

Unto mine, I will give to Him.
In the pastures of green, I lie awake,
Staring at the sky, envisioning Your Heavens,
With the angels at a chorus as one.

Oh Lord, I'm sure You know, down here is much division.
My heart aches for the ones not saved.
For they are bound by demons, Lucifer is never full.
Though, I have my soul, oh Lord.
They can afflict me, but they cannot kill me.

My heart sings to You, but it aches for what cannot be changed.
The pit is below, but Your Heavens are above.
If only they knew.

Oh Lord, what must I do? I love You so.
Let me not see me, but let me look to You.
Let my decisions be made by the fruit of You.
With You, Jesus Christ, I am but a child, pure as a baby.
In Your arms, I rest, in Your presence I am.

Let the fruitfulness multiply, oh Lord Jesus.
In my life, in their life, and in the lives to come.
The love shall increase, the joy shall emit.
The adventure shall come.
The excitement shall never end.

Dancing along the streams of Your Word, guided by Your hand.

Your fruits must follow me wherever I go,
with Your angels by my side as a covenant.

Light Overcoming the Dark

Rest thy eyes upon thy Father, He is a sweet goodness.
He has the sweet aroma that we long for.
Suffereth not, He has risen, and yet He will again.
He will come with the milk and honey overflowing as a sweet dove in the sky.

His beauty is everlasting, a soft embrace to the warm touch of a pondering heart.
Give, oh give, to Him all you long for and all you desire.
His heart is open if you desire.

The light will continue to shine on the other side,
But if you cross over, you will see it must shine inside.
Better it is to gather your fruit alone than to be dismayed at the rotten fruit displayed.
You will be stuck in a tragedy, and what you have gained will be lost if in the midst of the wrong partake.
You must go to the Man and give it up for His sake.

This one thing I may tell you,
Let love reign through in all you do.
Love comes from the heart, the heart pertains to life and death.
Let your heart be light of burden and hard to pain.
Cover it, but do not hide it, be vigilant in all you do.

Seek the Kingdom, and you will find what is gladly right.
The last thing you want to do is put up a fight.

But above all, let His light shine within you.
His light may overcome the darkness.

As you walk with Him, do not forget His power.
He carries authority above all the universe,
And through Him, darkness is cast out.

You may travel through the dark to understand the light.
Your heart must be made pure through the presence of His shine.

Contentment Is Met

The air carries on as a breath is pulled up.
The suction of the lungs holding onto breath, as one holding a mother's hand crossing an open street.
The thoughts pass through as the clock ticks.
You hold onto a few, keeping them from passing as cars on a freeway.
You stand watching your feet as the ocean lightly taps them with its cold touch.
Embracing the feeling that you were given, you laugh in awe.
Memories flow by as the waves clash, now and then,
Now and then.

Gratitude pours through your spirit for all the times given.
The creation created, the love that waged open.
The people that have stopped to cross your journey, the gifts that were given to you.
The perception that has dwelled within you.
All you know right now in this moment,
The ever-flowing of moments,
That one moment forms, preparing for the next.
You are not grieved by the idea that you know nothing; you are in awe.
You reason that you know this, only this. That is what brings you peace.
With this, you are content.

But oh, if you must, if you will, you will make the utmost.
You have the joyous of moments,
Because you know it will surely pass.
The precious suction of breath will surely ease.
You are content.

The Life of Creation Speaks

The sky lies awake at night, observing the land of the might.
They speak with the stars,
The trees blow as the wind rustles against life.
The life at hand will be brought to peace,
And the turmoil will be left behind.

As the faith increases,
Let not a seed grow that may wither your roots.
But let forth a seed that will prosper your might.
Continue to be led by His sight.
As you do, you will be moved with His great might.

The cries will come to a halt.
The thoughts will be proven guilty at the sight.
But look high, past the sky.
The winds talk, the trees commune, but the dirt is sacred.
For it was used on Adam.

This land was once holy, but it was rebellious.
What may come against a man is what has already come against God.
For if he is proud in the sight of Him,
Do you think he won't be proud in the sight of you?

Let not your heart wander,
Be steadfast and always in a mind of prayer.

The Lord Himself will see.
Follow Him, and you shall be.
Fear will cast out blessings, faith will cast out fear.
Oh nations, I ask of you, where is thy faith?
Let not your heart go weak but let Him be your strength.

Evermore and on, I write this to you.
Great joy shall fill the nations in due time.
The Lord did not go away; His hand lies in wait, ready to defend.
So oh, let Him fight for you, my friend.

The creation of God turned against Him,
To fill the temporal desire of pleasure from the spirits of fire.

Captured by Heaven

Capture it, my love,
Swing on that vine from above.
You will not be stopped once you continue.
His voice is strong; it cannot be heard by the weak.

You are doing what is needed to be led to be freed.
Your whisper was heard in the faint night.
Your cry did not go unheard.
Your steps were not crooked; they were being made straight.

Let them pass by, let not you cry, dear.
Let you be moved without fear, but let it be most clear,
That what you do, He sees too.
Where you cry, He will not let it be hidden, or pass as a lie.

But you will be forgiven, you will be blessed.
You will be held, and your heart will be caressed.
Forgiveness will overflow through you.
Grace will follow you.

You will lead many to the passage of your Father in Heaven.
Do not delay, do not hide, His voice is strong.
Let Him speak through you.
You will be a light for the ones in the darkness.

You will be a comfort to the weeping.
Love will be with you wherever you go, darling.

Keep flowing, keep showing, and keep going.
Never stop going till you reach your ever-flowing.

Time will come and time will pass,
Let it be so as you continue to flow.
Things come and go, but it will be for all to know,
That He is to come and never go.

Into the Light

I have a question. Did you make it?
After all those years, did you take it?
The light within you that needed your strength. Did you gain it?

Have you noticed your potential yet?
That you are stronger than you were conditioned to believe.
That there are no impossibilities, only the ones you create.
Would you know that to win is to not fight but to give?

That people come and go, but what they leave behind is what you need to continue to grow.
Hate is what you need to love stronger.
If you were not hated, how could you learn to fight?
How would you know that what they want is your light?

If you truly knew, would you turn and fight?
Into the sight of the light.
He is with you day and night.
Bathe in His peace, and He will feed your light.
You will not have to fight.

You can, if you must, fly out of sight.
Into the beauty of His might.
Continue on, fly high in the sky.
Leave a trace of your steps in the sand.

Shine His strength and give your fellows a hand.
Show them the way, the way that set you free,
That brought you home to be.
In His arms, you rest day and night.

Until the day comes, you will wait to take flight.
Lay here in the pastures of green,
Take what is yours, and don't be keen.
But be in awe.

Your Savior loves you so.
He brought you these gifts wrapped in a vintage bow.
Breath is His, and He has given you most, if not all, this...

Forbidden Love

Oh, if it may be.
Such a circumstance as this one,
All along, darling, it was all I wanted—to have fun.
A somber night, a heartless cry, one for the cold, one for the warm.

Two for the pantry boy, one for the flower girl.
A love, a tassel, a climb, a rebuked thought.
Caressing your mind.
A hope without a home.

A time without a clock in sight,
Leads me to the question: was your love ever in vain?
Did it ever stop without question?
Did you ever think about how your heart affected mine?

Your sickness colliding in my vine,
Oh, the overdrive was too much.
The circumstance was not hidden, but I know it should have been forbidden.
This I write with my heart in cry.

Deep down, I wonder, I wonder,
What's it like for a boy like you? Was it ever hard?
Of the river where it flew, write what you can, don't overdo.
Forbidden fruit. I have eaten it too,

Don't worry, it's not you.
That foul doing, I was timeless at the seams.
One day I will forgive.
But now, let me hold on. Before I let go.
She let go and let love.

Saved by Grace

So young but so old in spirit.
Wise or childish.
Mature or "immature."
Loving, always loving.
The ones that hurt her are the ones she guides.
She forgives.
She is light.
She is one with the world.
One with God.
One with herself.

Her laugh lets you see her beautiful spirit.
Her eyes show how much she's grown.
Her love shows how much she has in store.
She is a part of the world.
Her spirit is a child.
Her love is her gift.
Her heart is hers, well kept.
Her spirit is always shining.
Her mind is her root.
Her heart is the love.
Her spirit in the opening.
Her mouth is how she shows her spirit.
Her. She. Me.
I am all these things above.

With this, I hope you too can receive love.

A Moment of Transcendence

I have been feeling a level of discomfort from within.
I feel it's a sign of me once again transforming,
Opening another side of me that's been closed for a very, very long time.
It's old, and it's been waiting to be let out.

I never let myself feel this thoroughly because I've felt it was just something else that I could just let go,
But I cannot, and I'm okay with that.
This discomfort is an insecurity in some way, shape, or form.
I am fully transcending into a whole new version of myself.

Does this growth end? Or am I constantly going to be growing and molding in new shapes?
This is a new me. I am bright, lifting, and creative.
I am happy right now.
I don't want to change anything at this moment.
I am reminded that things change every moment, and I may feel differently with time.
And that is completely okay.

In a Moment's Time

Tomorrow is not promised; this moment is.
Use this moment to free yourself.
Give yourself to God.
God is the truest love you can ever find.
He is eternal; this life is not.
These people are not.

God loves.
Why do you not see? Are you sleeping?
Wake up, please. I am begging you.
You must give it all to Him.
You must leave sin behind.
It is not worth risking your life, risking your soul.

God is the most spiritual thing.
He is not a practice. He is not a ritual. He just is.
God is patient in love, as we should all be.
Forgive, brothers and sisters, and love everyone, because everyone is from God.
Some are controlled by their emotions or thoughts.

God is not.
God is holy and pure.
He is more than our minds can gravitate.

Trigger to Breath

I'm not running away anymore.
I'm facing my fears.
I was scared all these years,
Afraid of living to die.
I didn't want to say bye,
'Cause I knew that I was going.

I stopped confessing and started showing.
I put my life in God's hands.
I'm no longer afraid of a man.

He had a gun, and I started to run.
He was chasing me; he wanted more than I could give.
I just wanted to live.
God said, "You'll be just fine, you'll be alright."
I remembered—this ain't living if I'm spending my life runnin'.
He started shootin'.

Everyone was selfish, tryna save themselves,
'Cause they knew they were goners.
I stopped running, and I knew God had me.
Everyone started to flee.

He was behind me.
He pulled the trigger, and I felt my spine jerk.

I knew I was near death.

I fell flat, face first, and that was my last breath.

Opened my eyes,

Realized it was a dream, and got caught in the skies.

Receive His Light

I was running into the light.
My shadow was out of sight.
I was free. It was only me.

I let go of expectation,
Realized I could die at any minute.
But please recognize,
Nothing in this world is infinite.

The eternal lies in heavenly love,
But darling, remember, it comes from above.
Many lie in wait, not knowing they will soon meet their fate.
At one with the truth, they will be,
That love and the acceptance of the Father are what can set them free.

The chains of earth can only bring you down,
But His love will make you fly, singing heavenly sounds.
The green man is chased; he laughs and spits in your face.
If only you knew the greatest riches lie beneath,
I hope you would choose love,
'Cause darling, it'd be so keen.

As the sun sets, these physical matters are embraced.
The scattering mind is ever so clueless and worrisome,
Running into the traps of evil.

A puppet being played by the strings, as one runs into rings.
A rat running in place for the cheese that could not be reached.

Let not an item give you worth.
Embrace the Father who has made all creation in and over earth.
To love one another—
That is the greatest heart of birth.

The Doors Are Within

Time embraced,
A love you could not face.
With no holds, His love stretches out.

Beyond your sight,
You cower in the midst of your mire,
Not knowing what comes next is the great fire.
The holiest of holies,
The Alpha and Omega, Kingdom come.

For your life, darling, let it all go.
What is across, one day you may come to know.
For He wants you now, and the love of Him—oh, He loves you so.

Through the depths of your bone and the length of your spine,
He ever so yearns to shine.
Let you be brought with the truth, that what is yours is His.
What is His is yours.
Your spirit holds the Kingdom's doors.

A Hope Within

Mom, can you hear me?

I know the voices get loud.

As a child, I always wondered what made the family not stick around.

Your voice ruptured my heart at a young age.

I was writing poetry to heal the sick, page by page.

I found Jesus at seventeen,

It seemed your hate grew for me,

But maybe it was the demons not wanting to see.

The light burns the darkness.

My hope never ran out, I hoped you would overcome the lies of deception,

Feeding into you through demonic oppression.

If only you knew, Mother, that your worth never lied in a man but only in *the* Man.

I hope someday you can receive my love, I hope someday that you can.

I hope you heal before it's too late.

The dreams startle me as I wake up to the presence of you going into a quick fate.

Deep in your eyes lies the light,

You were afraid, so you blocked out His sight.

Time and time again, you refused love,

But I sure hope that someday you may receive it from above.

The Dark Sea of the Mind

Certain confidence is provoking.
As a wave swooshes in the sea,
You are distraught.

Brought again in the presence of a thought,
That what you are is what you think,
And what you think is what might make you sink.
Deep down in the dark blue ocean,
Your eyes shine bright,
Lighting up the night,
Without a caress in sight.
But only for a time, it would be in your mind.

If there were a God, there would be sight restored,
Healing to the sick,
Tending to the needy.
Your soul is desperate for the only Almighty.
You know of Him,
You don't know Him.
That thought grows you dim.

Your spirit is longing for the truth of all.
Where you are, you don't want it to make you fall.
You want the light, but you don't know of its shine or where it may hide.
Your thoughts wander in precision and delight.
In awe of what may be the greatest path of life in sight.

Your eyes pulled away, ever so afraid,
You heard a voice linger, "Take faith and take it by each grain, and one day I will be in your sight and remain."
You caught the breath of your tight lungs,
Pulled into a wave of the dark.
Engulfing, it made you quiver with each reach.
The push and pull of flesh and spirit,
The fear resisting faith.

Though you needed to swim,
Because you knew you desperately needed Him.

No other way there could be,
But to walk in the sight of His might.
It grew your spirit to walk by faith and not sight,
To strengthen you and gain your strength to fight the good fight.

Left Behind for Good

I ran the race at a moment's pace.
I did not look back, though I tried.
Everything of the past I left behind.

I would never forget your face when I said I was going to a new place.
A tear fell as I drove away.
There you stood, glancing to see if I'd change my mind and stay.
After a minute, you decided it'd be best if you walked away.
Leaving behind what was a disheveled play.

All along, I knew it wouldn't last.
Jesus called me to a place, and I couldn't let it pass.
Leaving it all behind was a decision I knew had to be made if I wanted to fly,
To live a life with Him on earth until I make my way back to the Highest skies.

So on I go, on we go, walking this walk of life,
Trying not to lose sight of the view of what we may pass.
Though I think and, at times, I cry of what may come and what will pass.

The Truth Being Revealed

You laugh as others scowl and leave a smell that is foul.
Your mind is filled with deceitful lies beyond man's time.
They wither away as you shed a tear in disgrace,
You were awed in heart until you left with a feeling out of place.

You dress in bright colors to hide the shame,
You laugh and sing as though you have nobody to blame.
But when you get home, you are distraught.
Brought to the mirror, you see who is not known.
What happened to the light? You ask yourself that every night.

Opening the page of your written story feels as though it's an act to a play.
You began to shake, and for the first time, what you felt could not be a mistake.
Tears streamed down each cheek as you were brought forth to the truth,
The clear reflection that what you are is not what you do, but it is *Him* who made you.

You fell to the ground, weeping.
In turmoil and distress, His Holy Spirit came with healing.
You now understand the prayers and the joy that comes from your mother who loves the Lord.
In a moment's pace, it all came to you that truth could not be

hidden,

And what is true shall forever be revealed.

Rest Upon Thy Rock

But those who are rich in spirit shall live everlasting upon thy firm rock.
The waters may flow of life, as the dove flies high above the sky carrying a message of peace.
The love of Him shall consume all that is His, and His peace shall be their take.

He gives unto you the greatest gift of love.
This you shall take and let spread like a wildfire,
Casting out all that is dark and making all that is His light.

With this, and with His, you will surely receive sight.
So wrap your arms within His majesty and receive His great might.
If the time may be now, give up the restless human fight.

For what will we take when we enter eternity?
The man of the earth holds his goods,
But the man of the spirit has understood.

That what is upon this earth shall come to pass,
But it is what's within the heart that will lead you to last.
The firm foundation of eternity will always be.
In His hands, you shall choose to sit, and He will let you see.

That what is to come is what you choose to be,
And what you make of this life shall pass onto the next.
So let it be fruitful and free.

So when the last tides come, you may rest upon thy rock of the Lord.

Like a Dove

Flying high above in the sky,
Soaring through the air with His might,
Regaining sight through the flight.

In midair, the grace falls from His wings high above,
You receive it and rise like a dove.
Gentle is your spirit and your touch,
You love and continue to give much.

With the guidance of Him, you are embraced as an innocent child.
You are renewed and restored from what was defiled.
With your wings spread open, you are gliding through the winds,
With love and peace as your compass, your light could never be dimmed.

Once you were drawn to the limitations of this earth,
But as you received His love, you were given a new birth.
A restoration for your spirit's flight,
A love to be rejoiced within the mind's eye.

Down below, you watch as much is taken for granted.
One scowls at the mire in the land, whilst you take in each molecule as grand.
Oh, how selfish and how plotful is the human spirit.

You wish all could feel His love and that it may give all a grand visit.

Like a dove, you sit up high,
Waiting peacefully in the sky for the right time to shine.

The Heart Is Your Greatest Treasure

The heart is your finest treasure. Hold onto it, dear,
For the Lord holds it close.
Don't fear the world, fear God.
Then you will find wisdom.
Your heart will then rise.

You will see that your love is your utmost treasure.
Oh, if you partake of His cup, you will see His mercies last forever.
Many may fall away, but know, upon you, His grace shall extend.
Everything wrong will be made right,
Everything dark will be brought into the light.

As your heart is transformed, let not a man tell you what he thinks is right.
But know the truth of God and let it set you free beyond any decree.
The man walks in his ways, but God knows all of his days.
For it is wise to store your heart in the hands of the Creator.

Your heart may die in your own hands,
For there is no source of light for it to be made pure.
For with God, you will flourish.
To your pain and hidden bondage, He will be the greatest cure.

Your Soul Shall Be Lifted

War starts in the mind.

What is dark will be revealed by His light.

Carry on with your heart.

Don't stop for a moment to glance at what was,

But come to the eternity of His love and let it be for us.

That what was, was, and what will be, will be.

But for the sake of your soul, have peace.

You are not this moment,

But the moment is a part played in the great atonement.

Your darkness shall be revealed,

Your heart shall be uprooted and appealed.

In the courts of His love, you shall be lifted high above.

Let not your tear cause you to self-corruption,

But let His mercy fill all of you to the greatest reparation.

A Point Is Still a Point

Wood or steel; a point is still a point.
Breath or death, a life is still a life.
As a mockingbird flies through the air of the sky,
It is the sheath opponent of one's soul.

Captivated by the mind's eye,
Lucrative a mind becomes as the breadth of the wind.
Through the somber, mischievous crescent moon,
The sky lies in wake night and day,
Who to devour once the body lets go and the soul becomes eternal.

Night and day,
The man looks on, on whom to pray.
Don't be scared, don't fray,
But have joy as the heart seems somber.
The stars shine bright as the supernova comes close,
Your mind lies in wake on what breadth to stay.

Let not your mind be in death, but receive the life of the day.
Joyous is His way.
Let Him continue as the way is made.
Through the darkest of nights,
Your soul shall meet the embrace of His light.

The Echo Into Eternity

The shockwaves of imprisonment linger in the mind,
For this causes a man to go mad.
But if one may be found, he may linger for the dark to find.

Oh child, your mother is not far; she is coming back.
Wipe your tears, from them arise life.
The closest are the furthest, the loveliest are the fakest.
Greatest is a fantasy in the mind that one creates for his mental sake.

Presumably for times of light so the dark could be disguised.
Times of suffering awaken the deepest starvation for joy.
Oh, it would be fun, wouldn't it?
To live in the hands of God,
So you may not need to create a definitive ploy for the hearts of the emptiest joy.

But you may receive what is real,
And finally, take part in all there is to feel.
Dance along with the joy in front,
You left it behind when you went shunt.
But now you remember, darling, that what was always will be.

It is in your mind that life is created, so continue to be free.
He is to be experienced first from within.
So let yourself first love, and all will echo into the present.

You will finally be with Him, and that will be the greatest heart of repentance.

The Light in the Life

Oh, what great joy to see the smiles on one's faces,
To be brought in an embrace of all the different races.
When love is met, all disappears.

The light reveals what is dark,
The light of another will surely make yours spark.
So come and rejoice, the Father is here, for He has always been near.
The light lives on through the passing of time, so lend your cheer.

Let us embrace in times of darkness so the light may reign,
His light is who we let shine through the pain.
I give thanks to love while in the dark,
For it is the mantle I walk with to the day of light, so I may not have a lasting mark.

Thanks we shall give to Him always,
In the darkest night, He will always shine,
My rock, my greatest vine.
I hold onto You so I don't run out of time.
I will receive Your light to shield the dark until my breath will meet its deadline.

Living with You is the greatest joy.
It is the embracement of life and light, overriding my selfish alloy.

You surely are the greatest light in the life, oh Lord of ours. With You is surely like a child running through a field of the most beautiful flowers.

The Sun Must Rise

Finally, there comes a time when the sun must rise.
After it all, you are met with losing your pride.
You are brought low.
Now you know, dear,
That what you are is what you chose to hear.

Let yourself be full of the greatest cheer.
The doors are open; the only prison was in your mind.
They almost made you believe you were out of time and out of line.

But Jesus has a way of loving through it all.
He led you through the mire,
He pulled you close to His fire.

Now you are being made one with His spirit,
Being led by His love lets you finally hear it.
The truth that was needed to embrace,
His hands are what guide you with His everlasting grace.

To be led by Him is the greatest joy of all,
For with Him, you can never fall.
With Him, the sun will always rise,
Especially inside.

The Vision Restored

I awoke, my eyes blinked for new sight.
The dream of the spirit held me up all night.
I twisted and turned,
The sun was beckoning for the day's return.

My body ached as my mind was out of state.
I sighed dimly at the pull ahead,
I got up, and the Spirit urged me to pray instead.

My eyes shot open as the dream came alive.
All of a sudden, I was lifted high, and my mind was revived.
Everything came clear at once.
What was not known was known.

What couldn't be paid for was received, and it clearly showed.
Now I had seen; my spiritual eyes were open.
In a second, I got what was never spoken.

Jesus paid the debt and met me in my sleep.
I knew from that time on, prayer would be my safe keep.
To recite His presence is the greatest gratitude of its essence.

The sight restored is the greatest treasure a man or woman
could ponder or abhor.
I now fly with the wind,
As the Spirit is being caressed from within.
Love keeps my sight clear.

His Spirit erases the fear and is now what I hold dear.
Prayer humbles the heart and frees your mind.
Let God have His place within you,
And let all that is old be made new.

The greatest of all, let your vision be restored too.

The Heart Is Your Greatest Treasure

The heart is your finest treasure. Hold onto it, dear,
For the Lord holds it close.
Don't fear the world, fear God.
Then you will find wisdom.
Your heart will then rise.

You will see that your love is your utmost treasure.
Oh, if you partake of His cup, you will see His mercies last forever.
Many may fall away, but know, upon you, His grace shall extend.
Everything wrong will be made right,
Everything dark will be brought into the light.

As your heart is transformed, let not a man tell you what he thinks is right.
But know the truth of God and let it set you free beyond any decree.
The man walks in his ways, but God knows all of his days.
For it is wise to store your heart in the hands of the Creator.

Your heart may die in your own hands,
For there is no source of light for it to be made pure.
For with God, you will flourish.
To your pain and hidden bondage, He will be the greatest cure.

Your Soul Shall Be Lifted

War starts in the mind.

What is dark will be revealed by His light.

Carry on with your heart.

Don't stop for a moment to glance at what was,

But come to the eternity of His love and let it be for us.

That what was, was, and what will be, will be.

But for the sake of your soul, have peace.

You are not this moment,

But the moment is a part played in the great atonement.

Your darkness shall be revealed,

Your heart shall be uprooted and appealed.

In the courts of His love, you shall be lifted high above.

Let not your tear cause you to self-corruption,

But let His mercy fill all of you to the greatest reparation.

A Point Is Still a Point

Wood or steel; a point is still a point.
Breath or death, a life is still a life.
As a mockingbird flies through the air of the sky,
It is the sheath opponent of one's soul.

Captivated by the mind's eye,
Lucrative a mind becomes as the breadth of the wind.
Through the somber, mischievous crescent moon,
The sky lies in wake night and day,
Who to devour once the body lets go and the soul becomes eternal.

Night and day,
The man looks on, on whom to pray.
Don't be scared, don't fray,
But have joy as the heart seems somber.
The stars shine bright as the supernova comes close,
Your mind lies in wake on what breadth to stay.

Let not your mind be in death, but receive the life of the day.
Joyous is His way.
Let Him continue as the way is made.
Through the darkest of nights,
Your soul shall meet the embrace of His light.

The Echo Into Eternity

The shockwaves of imprisonment linger in the mind,
For this causes a man to go mad.
But if one may be found, he may linger for the dark to find.

Oh child, your mother is not far; she is coming back.
Wipe your tears, from them arise life.
The closest are the furthest, the loveliest are the fakest.
Greatest is a fantasy in the mind that one creates for his mental sake.

Presumably for times of light so the dark could be disguised.
Times of suffering awaken the deepest starvation for joy.
Oh, it would be fun, wouldn't it?
To live in the hands of God,
So you may not need to create a definitive ploy for the hearts of the emptiest joy.

But you may receive what is real,
And finally, take part in all there is to feel.
Dance along with the joy in front,
You left it behind when you went shunt.
But now you remember, darling, that what was always will be.

It is in your mind that life is created, so continue to be free.
He is to be experienced first from within.
So let yourself first love, and all will echo into the present.

You will finally be with Him, and that will be the greatest heart of repentance.

The Light in the Life

Oh, what great joy to see the smiles on one's faces,
To be brought in an embrace of all the different races.
When love is met, all disappears.

The light reveals what is dark,
The light of another will surely make yours spark.
So come and rejoice, the Father is here, for He has always been near.
The light lives on through the passing of time, so lend your cheer.

Let us embrace in times of darkness so the light may reign,
His light is who we let shine through the pain.
I give thanks to love while in the dark,
For it is the mantle I walk with to the day of light, so I may not have a lasting mark.

Thanks we shall give to Him always,
In the darkest night, He will always shine,
My rock, my greatest vine.
I hold onto You so I don't run out of time.
I will receive Your light to shield the dark until my breath will meet its deadline.

Living with You is the greatest joy.
It is the embracement of life and light, overriding my selfish alloy.

You surely are the greatest light in the life, oh Lord of ours. With You is surely like a child running through a field of the most beautiful flowers.

The Sun Must Rise

Finally, there comes a time when the sun must rise.
After it all, you are met with losing your pride.
You are brought low.
Now you know, dear,
That what you are is what you chose to hear.

Let yourself be full of the greatest cheer.
The doors are open; the only prison was in your mind.
They almost made you believe you were out of time and out of line.

But Jesus has a way of loving through it all.
He led you through the mire,
He pulled you close to His fire.

Now you are being made one with His spirit,
Being led by His love lets you finally hear it.
The truth that was needed to embrace,
His hands are what guide you with His everlasting grace.

To be led by Him is the greatest joy of all,
For with Him, you can never fall.
With Him, the sun will always rise,
Especially inside.

The Vision Restored

I awoke, my eyes blinked for new sight.
The dream of the spirit held me up all night.
I twisted and turned,
The sun was beckoning for the day's return.

My body ached as my mind was out of state.
I sighed dimly at the pull ahead,
I got up, and the Spirit urged me to pray instead.

My eyes shot open as the dream came alive.
All of a sudden, I was lifted high, and my mind was revived.
Everything came clear at once.
What was not known was known.

What couldn't be paid for was received, and it clearly showed.
Now I had seen; my spiritual eyes were open.
In a second, I got what was never spoken.

Jesus paid the debt and met me in my sleep.
I knew from that time on, prayer would be my safe keep.
To recite His presence is the greatest gratitude of its essence.

The sight restored is the greatest treasure a man or woman could ponder or abhor.
I now fly with the wind,
As the Spirit is being caressed from within.
Love keeps my sight clear.

His Spirit erases the fear and is now what I hold dear.
Prayer humbles the heart and frees your mind.
Let God have His place within you,
And let all that is old be made new.

The greatest of all, let your vision be restored too.

Out of Place to Be in Place

I fell out of place,
Rearranged with time and space.
I'm wandering but not for long.

Questions arise,
How many until a part of me must die?
Is it me who is out of line?
Was I in sight but covered by the disguise?

I was yearning for more,
I got what I wanted across the shore.
Was I in a daze to forsake what could've been a mistake?
You were too much, my light was growing dim.

Now at last, I am to be with Him.
The Savior of my heart,
The Savior of all who adore the earth's art.
The Creator of time and just,
This was to be, it was a must.

Though at times my mind grows curious,
I know at last my spirit is in its place, not spurious.
So with this, I sit,
In the utmost content.

That time and peace are on my side,
Because He is on mine.

The Greatest Yoke

My body twists and turns,
I feel delirious with thoughts, my mind burns.
Shadows on the wall,
Paintings nailed on the wall begin to fall.

The floor begins to crack as a fire rises between,
Finally, what was known is now seen.
The screams from below are deafening.
As the light goes out, I begin to cower,

I start to cry out to the Lord,
It is not my time, and I need His power.
Tongues erupt from my mouth as my breath is pulled,
Time is going out, but before it does, I feel a rumble and hear a shout.

My eyes open, and I see it is He,
On a white horse with angels all around.
I am thrown back by His light.
He looks at me and pulls me up by His might.

"Thy Majesty, what shall I do to be rectified by Thee?"
"I say unto you, don't leave this light of mine but let it reign through in all you do."

My body fell back,
My eyes opened, and I noticed the floor had no crack.

The paintings were intact.
My mind was at ease.

For the first time, I was filled with His peace.
Though it was a dream, I know it was Him who spoke.
From that day on, I understand that between our breath and death lies the greatest yoke.

Forbidden Love

Oh, if it may be.
Such a circumstance as this one,
All along, darling, it was all I wanted,
To have fun.

A somber night, a heartless cry, one for the cold,
One for the warm.
Two for the pantry boy, one for the flower girl.
A love, a tassel, a climb, a rebuked thought.

Caressing your mind.
A hope without a home.
A time without a clock in sight,
Leads me to the question: was your love ever in vain?

Did it ever stop without question?
Did you ever think about how your heart affected mine?
Your sickness colliding in my life,
Oh, the overdrive was too much.

The circumstance was not hidden, but I know it should have been forbidden.
This I write with my heart in cry,
Deep down, I wonder, I wonder,
What was it like for a boy like you? Was it ever hard?

Of the river where it flew, write what you can, do what you can.

Forbidden fruit. I have eaten it too,
Don't worry, it's not you.
To get everything handed down.

To taunt your way into my days.
Into my dream.
To take what is mine and claim it as yours.
That foul doing, I was timeless at the seams.

You got too much to take of yours.
Possessive, mindless, taunting.
One day I will forgive.
But now let me hold on, before I let go.

The Romantic Heart

Time and time again, we fly, pulled into a caress.
A stop of the heart makes one lift.
My love, what is up there in your mind?
What is playing on repeat?

Is it me? Is it Him? Is it you?
Oh, what must I do?
I am so dearly in love with you.
How do you tell me?

I don't know, but if I can, I must fly.
You're beautiful, my love.
I don't care about the thoughts of others,
I know what I feel.

This feeling, oh this feeling,
I have not felt in ages.
Twice, my love, that is how much I have fallen for you.
But yes, if we must, if we shall, we will make a song.

We will sing it to the Heavens up above.
We will have our dance time and time again.
Around and around, we will spin on this earth.
With joy caressing our spirits,

With laughter easing the heart's presence.
Taking our time, breathing for this moment,

Dancing for this tick,

To you I say, my love,

Danke, meine Liebe, ich liebe dich sehr.

A Deceitful Love

What is the pull?
Dear, oh dearly, I have loved you for a time,
I have loved you for a season.
But to be with you, oh to be with you,

It scares me; yes, I drift.
This moment is all I feel, in its gaping sense.
No need to rush, nowhere to run, we are here,
Gifted from above.

Let us sit. Let us gaze at the stars.
Let us thank the Heavens.
It's our choice how fast or slow we want to move.
But with you, I wish to take my time,

To cherish the moment.

A Child's Path

Some children are given it all,
Whilst others must count their steps and try not to fall.
For if they do, getting up will be very hard.

You must be great, or you must work for the state.
The prison of lack will guide you off the longest track.
Lift up your head, my child, lift your burden up high,
Fall on your knees and leave it at His feet in the sky.

Lay down your fears,
For what it's worth, He will dry your tears.
Sit in His paradise,
And you will realize in Him is the greatest abide.

Passage of Prayers

This next part of this book contains prayers that were formatted to help aid anyone in their healing and walk with Christ. The greatest knowledge we can have in our walk with Christ is the importance of love and prayer. I hope these prayers help anyone in their walk with Christ or help deepen their understanding of prayer.

Before reading the prayers, I would like you to know the important factors that play a part in prayer:

Always repent for any sins before getting deep in prayer. Repentance is an act of turning to His light from darkness and receiving His goodness to turn from the darkness. Repentance clears the fog within you so that He may work within your heart deeper. Repentance is an act of receiving that you are in need of help and that He is your helper and Savior of your heart. **Read:** Acts 3:19, Matthew 3:2, 1 John 1:9, Matthew 9:13, Joel 2:12-13

Come to Him with thanks in prayer.
Giving thanks glorifies God as well as helps align us with His will. Giving thanks blocks out envy, bitterness, hatred, and more spirits of darkness. Giving thanks helps purify the heart by opening the heart to receive His love in a deeper way. In every season and time, giving thanks is of utmost importance. **Read:** Colossians 2:5-7, Colossians 4:2, Psalms 28:7

A Prayer for Restoration Through Brokenness

Lord, I know You are close to the brokenhearted.
You rest upon the shoulders of the soft-spoken.
You make all ways straight, Lord.
Your staff and rod are my comfort.
You restore all and make new what is old.

To You, Jesus, I turn my hope.
I lift my hands and bow my head.
I give thanks to You, Lord, for removing all that was in Your way.
To this moment, Jesus, I lift my eyes.
I give thanks, and I give You praise.
I lift my hands to the Heavens and begin to sing.
I know, Jesus, that You help me see.

Your Word is true and will never forsake me.
With Thy broken heart, I receive from You a brand-new start.
To You, Jesus, I give my burden to receive Your light.
I receive all that You have and accept Your might.
Thank You, Jesus, for this place so that I may be stronger for the next.

I know my brokenness is when You reign deeper,
And with that, I am brought closer.
I give thanks to You, Jesus.

The pain will be transformed into the greatest strength.

I will be a living example of Your Word and a testimony of its great truth.

Joel 2:25

"God can restore what is broken and change it into something amazing. All you need is faith."

A Prayer for Purity

Jesus, I know the experiences on this earth sometimes cause my heart to grow bitter.
But Lord, I pray that You guide me to receive Your love as an overflowing presence in my heart, washing out anything dark within me.
Let me not be defined or limited through the experiences or perceptions of others,
But let me be rooted in Your love.

Lord, let Your love purify my heart.
Let Your love be the root within my heart so that no darkness can overtake me.
Lord, if there is any part of my heart that is hard, bitter, and not receiving,
Guide me to let it go and let You take Your place deeper within me.

Let Your love shine through me.
Let me react with love to those who act with hatred toward me.
Let me be fully immersed in Your love so that my heart may experience You in a deeper way that is inconceivable at this moment.

Let me be fully immersed in Your love so that anything that has caused my heart to be hardened may be wiped away and I be made new in Your sight.

Let me receive the rebirth and restoration of my heart completely so I may walk more abundantly in Your light.
Let my heart not be a portion of the past,
But let it be completely new and filled with love, peace, and joy as a small child.

Let me come to You as a child, Lord Jesus,
For You said that if we do not come as a child, we will not know the Kingdom of Heaven.
Guide us to be born again, pure as a child within our hearts,
So what is spoken from our tongue will be heard by You,
And that we may see and experience You deeper without the fog of this human experience.

With this, Lord, let our love be genuine and always acted upon in every situation.
Let Your love be a guidance to our deepest healing of heart.
Let Your Holy Spirit wrap Your blanket of wisdom within us
So that we may walk strongly and boldly in Your name,
growing in purity and light within You.

Psalm 51:10

"Create in me a pure heart, O God, and renew a steadfast spirit within me."

A Prayer to Walk in Deeper Faith

Lord, sometimes I lose focus.
I get caught up in the pressures of life within society,
Which causes me to lose sight of Your Word and Your promises.
Sometimes I am caught up in what is logical or physically possible.

Jesus, I pray for deeper spiritual sight that leads me
To toss the physical realm to the side and live life on earth as in Heaven.
I receive Your guidance to be led more deeply by Your Holy Spirit.

I pray that everything dark within my heart is brought to the light
So that I may receive You more deeply.
As I receive You deeper, Lord, let me be moved by faith and not by sight.
Let my focus be restored as I read and meditate on Your Word.

Let my focus be within You and not this physical realm.
Let my focus be deeper within You so that what is seen falls away,

And what is of You is manifested around me through faith, love, and vision.

Proverbs 3:5-6

"Trust in the Lord with all your heart, and do not lean on your own understanding.

In all your ways acknowledge Him, and He will make straight your paths."

A Prayer for Restoration

Jesus, this earthly experience sometimes causes my light to be dimmed and darkness to grow within.
This causes me to lose my innocence and purity of heart.

Any trauma from my childhood, relationships, or ill words spoken over my life that may have hardened my heart in receiving You:
I pray for Your utmost love to overwhelm my heart and spirit so that everything that was taken from me (confidence, authority, leadership, speech, spiritual sight, love, forgiveness, etc.)
Is restored tenfold, and that I may be made pure in the sight of You, Jesus.

Any ill word spoken over my life, Jesus, I return them to the pit of Tartarus (Hell).
I receive Your Word over my life and Your promises.
I am not broken. I am not defined by my past.
Your love isn't measured by my acts.
Jesus, You love me the same today, tomorrow, and forever.

I receive Your love to restore and revive what was stolen and killed within me.
With this, Jesus, I receive Your guidance to fill me with a repentant, grateful heart
That may let Your glory shine through it all.

From this, Jesus, let me be a great testimony of Your great power and love.

Isaiah 61:7

"Instead of your shame, you will receive a double portion, and instead of disgrace, you will rejoice in your inheritance. And so you will inherit a double portion in your land, and everlasting joy will be yours."

A Prayer Against Self-Condemnation

I know if You have walked with others, You can walk with me.
Let me be receptive to Your love, and let me not condemn myself,
But let You be praised through it all.

Jesus, I know Your love isn't measured by my acts, but it is *who* You are.
Your love is what guides us to grow deeper within You.

For a long time, ill words were spoken over my life, Lord.
And to those whom I loved, I have only received hate.
Sometimes it causes me to feel as if I am not good enough,
That I am not worthy of Your love.

But I understand that this way of thinking can cause me to fall into deceiving darkness.
Jesus, I know I am not worthy of You, but let not that thinking hinder my receiving of You.
Lord, You said there is no condemnation in Christ Jesus.
I am free from my sin since I am walking with You.

I am not defined by my past.
I am defined by Your love and Your Word.
Let me walk completely in love for myself and others through You.

Guide me through fasting and prayer to cut any bondage from spirits of darkness
That are speaking around and within me through others and through me.
Lead me to study Your Word deeper
So that I may walk in confidence in You, Jesus,
So that I may not walk in condemnation but receive the complete freedom of You.

Thank You, Jesus. You are a wonderful, beautiful God.
You have created everything beautiful in its time, including myself.

Romans 8:1-2

"Therefore, there is now no condemnation for those who are in Christ Jesus, because through Christ Jesus the law of the Spirit who gives life has set you free from the law of sin and death."

Prayer for Unity

In deep concern, I may be in,
For the world, for the church, for myself.
But what centers my concern, Jesus, is unity.

It is far too common for there to be a lack of peace.
Jesus, it has gotten suffocating.
The world is not unified; we are divided.

Jesus, belief has divided us, religion has divided us,
Pain has ultimately separated us.

In this prayer, Jesus, I pray for unity.
I pray, Lord, that Your love reigns,
And that instead of religion being pressured,
Let Your love be radiant and ever-flowing to those all around.

Fill us with a desire to be closer to You.
Let a desire for Your love uproot within us so that we may shine with Your love.
Let Your love shine through us so much that it bridges every gap,
That every division is unified by Your love,
And every difference is forgotten through the abundance of Your love being received within us all.

2 Corinthians 13:11

"Finally, brothers and sisters, rejoice! Strive for full

restoration, encourage one another, be of one mind, live in peace. And the God of love and peace will be with you."

Prayer for Authenticity in the Church

Lord, church doesn't feel like church sometimes.
I see more exchanges of business than worship in Your name, Lord.
I receive Your guidance to open my spiritual eyes
To see whether the church is glorifying You or themselves.

I want to see more of Your truth.
I want to see Your love reigning through the church.
At times, it feels like a facade sitting below the altar.
How many are truly in love with You?

Open my eyes so that I may see Your love in the church.
Guide me to discern whether the church is rooted in Your love or self-seeking.
I pray that the church leaders are led by Your Holy Spirit
And filled with Your presence, Jesus.

Guide their tongues to speak the complete truth and authenticity of You
So that souls are not led astray.
Let them display Your Word and not just speak it.

I pray for the hearts that are lacking faith
Due to the speakers of the church not carrying out Your love.
I pray for church trauma to be healed for those who experienced a deceitful light of You

That has led them astray from faith.
Let them experience Your agape love, Jesus.

I pray for Your truth to be revealed and for the veil to be lifted completely
So that Your Holy Spirit has its utmost way in the church.
Let every church leader and speaker be comfortable to come as they are,
To remove the mask and accept themselves as they are
To receive You to work within them completely, Lord.

I pray for the religious spirits to be revealed
So that a new revival may be declared in Your name through every church across the nations, Jesus.
For the truth to be revealed all across the nations,
Displaying the power of Your love.

Let the veil be lifted so we may experience Your love more abundantly in the church.
We receive You more abundantly in the church, Jesus.
Thank You, Lord.

Galatians 1:10

"Am I now trying to win the approval of human beings, or of God? Or am I trying to please people? If I were still trying to please people, I would not be a servant of Christ."

Prayer for Those Carrying Burdens of the Past

Oh Jesus, I have experienced a lot.
It has caused my heart to ache with the pain of the past.
It has caused my sleep to be stolen and my dreams to be shaken, waking my spirit in shivers.

I have dealt with fear for long enough, my spirit is tired of bearing a useless burden.
My body aches, although I still pray.
I desperately search for You with my mind in torment.
I read Your Word, and my heart lifts for moments before I am met with the reality of my circumstance.

Questions arise as I yearn for You:
Are You there? Are You listening? Do You still love me?

Oh God of this universe, guide my soul, spirit, mind, and heart
To break these chains and bondages of my past and the lies that creep into my mind.
Lead me to walk in Your light, to take control of this moment, of what is now.

Lord, Your Word says to not boast about tomorrow,
For we do not know what a day may bring forth (Proverbs 27:1).
Let me not worry about the next moment, let me sit in this moment.

Guide my focus to be aligned with the now,
To receive the newness of Your grace and Your mercy every morning.
Guide and mentor my spirit to fully receive the light of You
That I may walk in Your light and not the shadow of my past.

Let me let go of the burden of my past to receive You completely.
Your Word says that we are free in You, Jesus,
And there is no condemnation for those who are in You, Lord (Romans 8:1-2).

So guide me to fully receive the freedom of Your love,
To walk in Your light and the newness of this moment.
Thank You, Lord.
I receive what I can receive in this moment from You,
For You to do Your work within me.

I receive You to continue to heal me from within
And to receive control of the now
So that You can have Your way fully within me,
And for me to walk in Your light and newness.

Matthew 11:28-30

"Come to me, all of you who are weary and carry heavy burdens, and I will give you rest.
Take my yoke upon you. Let me teach you, because I am humble and gentle at heart,
And you will find rest for your souls."

A Prayer for the Lonely

Lord, sometimes it gets lonely.
It gets harder to meet people and connect with people as I get older.
I yearn for You, but the closer I get to You, the lonelier I feel.

I know that may be the veil being lifted so Your will may have its way,
But at times, my thoughts echo, and my mind reflects on what I lack.

Lord, I pray for those who feel empty and misunderstood,
Remind them that You hear their cry, that You are closer to them.
Jesus, You know their heart, You know what they need.
I pray, Lord, that You guide them and fill their hearts with Your love.
Restore every area of their life with Your abundance of peace, joy, and love.

That in times of darkness, Lord,
Shine Your light on them through others, through experiences, and encounters.
Let them experience Your agape love, Lord.
I pray that loneliness turns into joy and fulfillment.

Let them know, Jesus, that they are not alone,
For You have gone through loneliness on the cross.

You went through loneliness in the desert while You fasted for forty days, Jesus.
You know our pain, Lord.

Remind us that we are not alone in feelings of loneliness.
You are with us in the depths of our hearts and spirits.
Remind us of Your truth, Your Word, and fill us with Your love
So that every area of darkness and emptiness is filled with Your light.

John 14:18-21
"I will not leave you as orphans; I will come to you.
Before long, the world will not see me anymore, but you will see me.
Because I live, you also will live.
On that day, you will realize that I am in my Father,
And you are in me, and I am in you.
Whoever has my commands and keeps them is the one who loves me.
The one who loves me will be loved by my Father,
And I too will love them and show myself to them."

Prayer Against Abuse

If you are dealing with abuse or you have dealt with abuse in the past,
I would like you to know that I have as well, and you are not alone.

If the Holy Spirit pulls you to, repeat this prayer against abuse:

"Lord, in this prayer, I pray against abuse.
You have set me free in Your name, and by Your blood, I am living a new life.
Every ill word, action, and slander done against me to cause harm
And bring destruction upon my life, I return it back to the sender.

I am who You say I am, Jesus.
I declare and decree that the healing of You shall take place within my heart, mind, and spirit.
I receive Your agape love to transcend my mind and spirit, surpassing my understanding.

Every curse that was spoken over my life through an ill tongue,
I rebuke it in Jesus Christ's name, and I send it to the pit of Tartarus.
I take authority over my life,
And I declare that I am not a shadow of abuse,

But I am a strong, vibrant warrior in Your name,
With Your light shining through me.

I take authority over this atmosphere of mine,
And I call on the angels of Your heavenly places to take my case
And be my spiritual backup
As I move from the darkness of my past into the present of Your light.
I receive Your love, Lord.

In Jesus' Mighty Name, I pray, amen."*

Proverbs 22:10
"Drive out a scoffer, and strife will go out;
Quarreling and abuse will cease."

Prayer for Grace

My heart feels heavy at times,
Weighed down by the apathy taking place around me.
It causes me to wonder:

"Could I get like that? Could I be so cruel?"

When someone does something to me, Jesus,
I think to myself:

"I could never do that to them. How could they?"

But Lord, I then remember how You traveled far distances
To heal, restore, and embrace those who yearned for You.

There were so many religious folk who were against Your teaching and ministry,
But You still healed, You still traveled,
And You never gave up, Jesus.

Until Your last breath on the cross,
You still cared for others (Luke 23:34).

You had so much grace, Jesus,
Even when You were stoned, persecuted, and beaten.
Lord, I pray that You continue to work in our hearts
And mend our spirit to let us carry more of Your grace.

Let us walk in grace as You have.
Let us receive so much of Your love

That grace overflows within us,
And everything You are shines through us.

Let the grace of You have its way within us, Jesus,
And give us the strength to continue to pray
And fight against bitterness, greed, and selfishness.

Let our output not intend to match the flow of others,
But let it be a complete, genuine reflection of Your love uprooting within us.

Let us act in love, kindness, patience, and grace, no matter what.
Guide us to be discerning of our own hearts
And lead us with the wisdom of You
So we may walk in Your love and grace,
Letting Your Word be displayed through our actions and words.

Thank You, Jesus.
In Jesus Christ's name, I pray.

John 1:16

"Out of His fullness, we have all received grace in place of grace already given."

"And this is the confidence that we have toward Him, that if we ask anything according to His will, He hears us. And if we know that He hears us in whatever we ask, we know that we have the requests that we have asked of Him."- 1 John 5:14-15

Prayer for Self-Love

At times, it is hard to see myself as You see me, and I have learned that only makes it difficult for You to work through me completely.
The burdens of my past and my sin weigh heavy at times, making it hard for me to accept and love myself in the way You describe me.

Lord, guide me to accept the love of You within me.
Let me walk in the identity of being Your child and not in the identity of my actions.
Teach me, Jesus, that I am just a human, and yes, I mess up, but that does not define me.
Past abuse does not define me—You define me, Lord.

I know this, but at times, my heart is hard to receive Your truth due to my focus being caught in the physical realm.
Move my eyes to Your Heavens, Jesus—to Your Kingdom—so I may not be caught up in physicality, but so that I may live on this earth as in Heaven.

Guide me to keep my focus on You, meditating on Your Word day and night
So that my heart may receive Your complete love,
So my heart may walk in how You call me to walk completely—
In love for myself and love for others completely.

Let me see myself as You have created me.

Guide me to the understanding and mentoring of my spirit

So I may focus on the eternity of You rather than the temporal vanity of my body and this earth.

As I walk in Your truth, Jesus, let every insecurity, self-resistance, self-hatred, and ill word spoken over myself fall away,

And let the love of You wash over me so I may accept love for myself.

Let me know how to tend to my own heart, mind, and spirit without manipulation, deception, and the lies of others.

Have Your way within me completely, Jesus,

So I may boldly walk in Your truth, bearing self-love,

So I may discern deception, attack, and anything of darkness coming between Your light for me.

In Jesus Christ's name, I receive Your love to guide me to self-love and boldness in Your name.

Amen.

Matthew 22:40

"Love the Lord your God with all your heart and with all your soul and with all your mind.

This is the first and greatest commandment. And the second is like it: 'Love your neighbor as yourself.'

All the Law and the Prophets hang on these two commandments."

Prayer Against Manipulation

They call it gullible, push-over, "too nice." But Jesus, I just love.

Does a loving heart always have to leave an open door for attack?

Am I too nice, Jesus?

Why do some make it seem like Christians always have to have a smile and act as if nothing bothers them?

Isn't that fake, Lord?

In the end, doesn't it just leave us open for manipulation?

Small Testimony and Prayer:

Time and time again, I have experienced manipulation.
But I have learned it was due to my lack of discernment,
setting boundaries, and not taking authority in Your name.

You say it plainly in the Bible, Jesus, that we shall walk boldly,
That we may stand against the schemes of the devil (Ephesians 6:10-18).
I had mistaken Your Word for a happy, sunshine movie play,
And not the reality of the walk with You for a while.

I nitpicked Your Word according to what my heart wanted to receive at the moment.
But now, Jesus, I understand that we must wear Your whole armor—not just a portion.
Nitpicking Your Word, Jesus, has only left me open for attack.
In my case, it left me open for manipulation.

I did not cover myself with You fully, and that led me to get hurt.
I was not honoring Your Word completely.
I didn't fully guard my heart since I was not completely obeying Your truth.
I took small portions of Your Word and tried to cover my

whole body, mind, and spirit with it,
But it was only meant to cover a portion.

I focused too much on the importance of love and giving,
And I lost focus on the schemes of the devil and how deceiving they are.
Little did I know, Jesus, that would lead me to be fooled by many,
Robbing my peace and my faith in You due to my lack of knowledge.

I know now, Jesus, that it was merely my fault, and Your truth has always been true.
It was I who made the mistake of not taking Your Word absolutely seriously.

I pray, Jesus, for those who deal with manipulation due to lack of knowledge,
Lack of self-control, lack of confidence, etc.,
That they may come to the full acceptance of Your truth.

Yes, we are to walk in love, but that doesn't mean
We have to push ourselves beyond what we can handle
And beyond what we are comfortable with to please others.

Guide us to walk in authority, set boundaries,
And walk in Your truth with the boldness of You around us.

Let us walk in complete knowledge of Your truth
So that we may be discerning of the schemes of the devil and

his fallen hierarchy (demons and evil spirits),

And we may guard our hearts.

In Jesus' name, I pray.

Proverbs 4:23

"Above all else, guard your heart, for everything you do flows from it."

Prayer for Strength

The burden is too much, Lord. I have lost control.
My spirit is weak; my heart is sinking. How far has love gotten me?
It has gotten me to the point of weakness. I have given much only to lose more.

I need Your strength, Lord. I need Your breath within my lungs because I am afraid mine is afar.
I am losing sight, I am losing might. I cannot take this trouble of being broken, of losing this strand of life.
I know I must let go, that holding on is only making my bones ache ever more.

There is more to this pain, I know. You have more for me, Jesus—you must.
I feel I am done, but You are not. I must be done for You to start.
I cry day and night, my heart wallows in heaviness. The desperation for more is too much to bear.

Guide me to receive Your strength, Jesus, to receive Your strength surpassing my limited conception.
I know I must not wallow in myself; I must fully die for You to live.
I receive Your strength to have its way in me completely so my bones may be filled with Your blood,
Giving me new life, sight, and vision.

This heaviness only reflects my humanness and my utter weakness as a human on this earth that is vanity.

With that knowledge now, Jesus, I know I must receive Your strength

To renew my bones and lift my heart of all burden.

I must move my eyes from my weakness to the acceptance of Your strength.

Guide me to receive Your strength, Lord,

To cast out my weakness more and more every day so You reign within and around me.

In Jesus' name, I pray.

Isaiah 40:31

"But they that wait upon the Lord shall renew their strength; they shall mount up
with wings like eagles; they shall run, and not be weary; and they shall walk, and not faint."

Prayer for Your Truth to Be Revealed

There is much deception all around, Lord.
I know if I do not stay steadfast in a mindset of prayer and meditation on Your Word,
I can be caught in a snare of lies, false reality, demonic bondage,
A spirit of self-seeking, and much more—even beyond what I may conceive.

I do not want to live a lie, Jesus.
I don't want to live out of line with Your will and truth.
I don't want blinders on—I want the truth.
I want what is real, what is Your complete will.

Anything that is within or around me that may be a lie or false reality,
I ask, Jesus, shine Your light so the veil may be lifted and so Your will may be done.
Any person, habit, thought, or word that I am surrounding myself with, Jesus,
That is not aligned with the complete truth of You,
I ask that You reveal it to me so that I may know how to move according to Your will.

I receive Your guidance for me to move away, destroy,
And cast out anything in my life that is not of You and Your

truth.

Guide me to the wisdom and understanding of Your truth
So I may take the steps into moving according to Your will.

I receive You to have Your way, Jesus, and shine Your light.
Thank You, Lord, I receive Your will and truth.

In Jesus' name, I pray. Amen.

Luke 12:2-3

"For there is nothing covered that shall not be revealed; neither hidden, that shall not be known."

Prayer Before Sleep

Thank You, Jesus, for carrying me throughout this day to make it to nighttime.
As I begin to rest my body, Jesus, I call on the atmosphere of Your angels
And Holy Spirit to protect my mind, body, and spirit.

I ask, Lord, that You guard my sleep with peace and restoration
So I may wake up refreshed in an atmosphere of Your love and peace.
Let Your angels and Holy Spirit guard my space where I lay my head,
So that my sleep is not interfered with by anything not of You.

I cancel out spirits of fear, stress, and anger
So my sleep is not interrupted with evil.
If You have a message for me,
Speak to me tonight through my dreams
And let not any evil spirits hinder Your message for me through my sleep.

I cover my mind, body, and spirit in the blood of You,
Surrounded by Your peace to guard me.
I love You, Jesus. Thank You. Amen.

Psalm 4:8

"In peace I will lie down and sleep, for You alone, O Lord, make me dwell in safety."

Prayer Against Ungodly Thoughts

My thoughts wander at times.
I catch myself in unlikely scenarios that are not aligned with Your goodness.
These thoughts sometimes cause me to lose focus on Your truth.
I get caught in deception of my own making, of my own leading.

At times, there are whispers—whispers in my ear to do against Your will.
I cast these thoughts not of You to Tartarus (hell),
I send them back to the sender in Jesus Christ's name.

I declare and decree the enemy has no stronghold,
No power, no authority within my mind.
By the blood of Jesus, I am set free.
I will not be a captive in deception, lies, and mockery.

I receive Your guidance to help me turn my mind to You, Lord,
To yearn deeply for Your goodness
And the renewal of my mind by Your love and Your grace.

I receive Your Holy Spirit to uproot anything in my mind not of You, Jesus.
Thank You, Jesus.

In Jesus' name, I pray.

Philippians 4:8

"Counter negative thoughts with God's Word and speak His truth."

Prayer to Forgive

My heart is burdened with the things done against me.
It wallows in the question of *"Why me?"*
Aren't I deserving of better?
What have I done to receive such treatment?

But Jesus, I remember—
There is too much *"I"*, too much *"me"* involved in my questions.
When I take a look at the bigger picture,
I remember it is not just me;
Others have similar experiences.
It is very egotistical of me to think of myself as such a victim and as innocent.

If You have forgiven me, that means I can forgive others.
I am not perfect, they are not either.
I know what was done to me was wrong,
But I am only hurting myself if I continue holding on.

To receive Your love, Jesus,
Is to let go of the burdens of anguish within being wronged.
It is difficult to carry the burden of hurt and bitterness.
I am learning, Jesus, that it is even harder to continue carrying it than to let go.

Jesus, I ask that You guide me to forgive,
Guide me to let go.

It is not my burden to carry.

I must forgive, although I know it is hard.

Lord, I choose to shift my focus
To receiving Your love, to receiving Your renewal,
And to let everything of Your will be done.
I receive Your guidance within my heart—letting go and forgiving.

Thank You, Jesus. Amen.

Matthew 6:14

"For if you forgive others their trespasses, your heavenly Father will also forgive you."

Prayer Against A Cursing Tongue

Cursing is all around me. At times, it's all I hear in my mind when I am upset or distressed.
Your Word says that we must refrain from belittling talk. (Ephesians 4:29)

So Jesus, guide me to the renewal of my tongue so that my tongue will speak of life and not death—to myself and to others.
You have taught me, Jesus, that a tongue brings life or death and that cursing can bring death spiritually, mentally, or physically.
Sometimes, cursing spills out of my mouth as easily as water being spilled when it gets knocked over.

Lord, I ask that You guide me to grow in self-control, self-awareness, and discernment to guard my mind and my tongue. Let my tongue and mind not be manipulated by this world but let them be transformed by You and Your Heavens.
Let my tongue be guided by Your angels and Holy Spirit to speak sweetly and gently and not foul with corruption.

I receive Your angels and Holy Spirit to guide my tongue to speak with sweetness, goodness, grace, and understanding—With the fruits of patience, self-control, and self-awareness guarding and guiding my tongue and mind as I speak.

In Jesus Christ's name, I pray. Amen.

Proverbs 18:21

"The tongue has the power of life and death, and those who love it will eat its fruit."

Prayer for Uplifting Friendship/Relationship

Lord, You have taught me that friendship impacts one's growth and character.
Friendship is as close as a brother, sometimes closer than blood.
I pray, Jesus, that my friendships are uplifting and beneficial in my walk with You and on this earth.

Let my friendships radiate in the fruits of You—with love, patience, forgiveness, gentleness, and kindness.
Let any friendship that is not of You and in the way of Your will fall away.
Guide me to grow closer to the friendships that are aligned with You and further from the ones that are not aligned with You.

Reveal Your truth through my friendships, Jesus.
I receive Your guidance through my friendships and Your wisdom to guide me
On how to get closer to Your will and further from deception.

I receive Your guidance to grow in discernment as well as being obedient to Your voice.
Any friendship or relationship that is not uplifting me or increasing me in my walk with You,
I ask that You guide me to uproot it while restoring my

spiritual vision and discernment

So that I may know how to walk in Your light and not be impacted by darkness.

I love You, Lord.

Let Your will be done, in Jesus' name. Amen.

Proverbs 18:24

"A man of many companions may come to ruin, but there is a friend who sticks closer than a brother."

Prayer Against Pride

Lord, You oppose pride and give grace to the humble.
If there is any pride in me, Jesus—any religious pride, any worldly pride—
Guide me to uproot it by the blood of You.

Humble my spirit, Lord, so that I may not walk proudly, but so that I can walk humbly in Your name.
Guide my ego to be shed for Your Spirit to be completely uprooted within me, Jesus.
Let me be in prayer on my knees more, so that my spirit may be humbled by the presence of You.

I am Your sheep, Jesus, and You are my Shepherd.
I receive Your guidance for every ounce of pride to fall away so that I and other souls are not led astray by my pride.
Cover my whole body, mind, and spirit with Your power and Your authority so I am brought low.

If I must, Jesus, let me fall so I may be humbled and my pride may be altered and dispersed into praise and humility.
Let me fall away so You can take Your place.
I am just a mere speck of dust for a short while on this earth, You are forever and eternal, Jesus.
I receive Your guidance in humbling my spirit.

Thank You, Lord. Have Your way.
Amen.

Proverbs 11:2

"When pride comes, then comes disgrace, but with humility comes wisdom."

Prayer for Self-Control

I am in conflict with my flesh and spirit, desiring for You to reign.
Lord, I give You permission to reign within me.
Guide me to not fall into temptation but to receive Your Holy Spirit and have its way within me
So Your fruits may shine through this temple of Yours, which is my body and spirit.

I know we may never be perfect; temptation will never fall away.
But Lord, through You, I know I am strong enough to face these fleshly and earthly battles
By receiving You to reign within me.

Guide me to think before I do or say anything—
To evaluate my actions and words, as well as control what kind of person I reflect onto others.
Guide me toward the fruit of self-control and the knowledge of how self-control can aid my spirit and body in the long run.

Pleasure is temporal, but good fruit is eternal.
I receive Your guidance to mentor me through self-control
And the knowledge as well as the understanding that may come with it.

I receive Your teaching and Your guidance for a fruitful character to reign within me.

I cancel out anything I have done or said through lack of self-control in the past,
And let it not hinder my decision-making in the present moment.

I receive the newness of this moment that is stored in Your grace and mercy,
For good change to be planted within me.

Thank You, Jesus. I love You.

1 Corinthians 10:13

"No temptation has overtaken you except what is common to mankind. And God is faithful;
he will not let you be tempted beyond what you can bear. But when you are tempted,
he will also provide a way out so that you can endure it."

Prayer Against Selfish Desire

I get wrapped in my own wants and desires, losing track of what You will.
My eyes shift to the reflection of myself instead of Your Kingdom.
My mind keeps track of my own goals and plans, not second-guessing if it is what You will.

I am brought low when my own wants and desires only lead me to failure and blindness in vision.
I think I know what is good for me until I have it, and I am only left with a deeper understanding of the limitations of the human mind—
That I may not know what I need because I am entangled with self-importance, selfish desire, and temptations of pleasure daily, Lord.

I pray against getting caught in selfish desire that would only hinder Your will.
I know, Jesus, that the only person that can hinder Your will is me.
Pull me closer to Your will and Your calling for me and further from my own.
My will is temporal, but Yours is everlasting through

generations.

Pull me deeper into what You desire for me, Lord.

Let me keep in prayer and meditation daily on Your Word and Your goodness,
Giving thanks and praise to You before I rise and before I sleep.
I know Your will aligns with what is good for me and what is fulfilling for me,
So let You reign through me, Jesus.

Decrease me so You can increase.
Let everything I do bring me closer to You and glorify Your will.
Guide me to serve others selflessly.
Let me practice listening to others deeply and intently.
Shine through me with Your love so others can see You through me.

I receive Your love and guidance through the decreasing of myself
So Your Spirit and will can reign through me and through my plans and visions for the future and present.

I love You, Jesus.
Thank You, Lord. Amen.

Ecclesiastes 4:4
"And I saw that all toil and all achievement spring from one

person's envy of another. This too is meaningless, chasing after the wind."

Prayer Against Self-Victimization

Conflicts occur, sometimes more often than not.
These conflicts arise within, a battle between the self, interfering with my walk with You.

Lord, I know I may be a victim, and yes, I may have been abused, treated badly,
And put down in ways I could not understand.
But giving my life to You, Jesus, has taught me that things are different,
And I can live in freedom with You.

I am not a shadow of my past.
Lord, let the traumatic experiences of the past not hinder this moment.
I accept what has happened, and I know that it is only myself
That can pull me into darkness henceforth.

Diminish self-victimization from me, Jesus.
Let me bathe in Your love and Your wing so that I may be a living testimony of Your great power.
Not everyone is against me.
I am not perfect.
I am not the center of attention.

Let me see others in Your light and not in the shadows of my past experiences.

Let me receive a new heart, mind, and spirit within You, Jesus.

Let me not live within the worldly standard and culture,
But let me live by Your Word with Your love and Spirit.

I thank You, Jesus.
I receive Your guidance to walk in Your light henceforth.
I love You, Jesus.
Amen.

Psalm 71:20

"Though You have made me see troubles, many and bitter, You will restore my life;
from the depths of the earth You will again bring me up."

Prayer for A Spirit-Led Day

Thank You for giving me this new day and breath in my lungs.
Thank You for guarding my sleep with angels and Your Holy Spirit,
Guiding me to have a peaceful, restful night.

I cover this day with Your angels and Holy Spirit to guide me and guard me, Lord.
Guide me to fulfill what You have in store for me today, Lord.

Let all I do today be filled with the fruits of Your Holy Spirit:
Love, patience, kindness, forgiveness, selflessness, joy, peace, self-control, and gentleness. (Galatians 5:22)

I receive Your covering and guidance for this day.
If I am not in a place of fully receiving You within this moment,
Guide me to receive You fully today.

Thank You, Jesus.
I love You. Amen.

Psalm 143:10
"Teach me to do Your will, for You are my God;
may Your good Spirit lead me on level ground."

Thanking Jesus

Thank You, Lord, for guiding me this far.
This moment is proof that Your strength endures forever.
Your grace rests upon my soul, and I thank You so much for Your eyes on me.
For the hand of You that rests upon my spirit, mind, and body.

Thank You for humbling me so that I may reach others through Your love.
The greatest thing one can do is love, and I thank You for mentoring me on the importance of love.

Thank You, Jesus, for being my Father when I had none.
Thank You for being my closest friend when I felt alone.
Thank You for guiding me out of toxic situations
That were only hindering my walk with You.

Thank You for Your strength reigning through me.
Thank You for never losing sight of me and for always hearing my prayers.
Thank You for listening and for caring about me.
Thank You for pushing me every day to be better.
Thank You for people, for connections, for opportunity.

Thank You for this life, this breath, this very moment I am able to feel.
Thank You for food, water, shelter, and protection.
Thank You for always guiding me through the days with Your

Spirit and angels.

Thank You for watching over my loved ones.

Thank You for Your never-ending forgiveness.

Thank You for Your grace that is new every morning.

Thank You for community, for self-improvement, for love, for restoration.

Thank You for restoring and strengthening my soul, surpassing what I can conceive.

Thank You for the lessons time and experience have taught me.

Thank You for wisdom, knowledge, and truth.

Thank You for Your presence, Lord.

I love You. Amen.

1 Thessalonians 5:16-18

"Rejoice always, pray continually, give thanks in all circumstances;

for this is God's will for you in Christ Jesus."

www.ingramcontent.com/pod-product-compliance
Lightning Source LLC
LaVergne TN
LVHW061549070526
838199LV00077B/6960